How to survive children

This is not a book about how to bring up your children properly; there are too many of them already. Childcare is a growth industry with half a million teachers, eight thousand health visitors, the National Children's Bureau and uncounted numbers of academics all toiling away on how children develop, how their teeth form, why they don't learn to read, what must be done to rid them of psychosis and nits. Scarcely a day goes by without another book on Children's Rights or Your Wonderful Baby.

It's the rights and needs of parents I'm concerned about; the battered consumers of all this expertise. For since the one thing they're all agreed about is that children are wonderful, then everything that goes wrong must be our fault. I blame Rousseau, myself: all this stuff about the nobility of the savage child, which could only be tainted by rotten old civilised us. Man is born free, indeed! Man is *not* born free — he is born attached to his mother by a cord and is incapable of looking after himself for at least seven years (seventy, in some cases).

KATHARINE WHITEHORN
HOW TO SURVIVE CHILDREN

with drawings by
BILL BELCHER

MAGNUM BOOKS
Methuen Paperbacks Ltd

A Magnum Book

HOW TO SURVIVE CHILDREN
ISBN 0 417 03200 5

First published in Great Britain 1975
by Eyre Methuen Ltd
Magnum edition published 1978
Reprinted 1979

Text copyright © 1975 by Katharine Whitehorn
Drawings and captions © 1975 by Bill Belcher
Cover Copyright © 1977 by Norman Thelwell.
Illustration taken from Thelwell's *Brat Race*,
published by Eyre Methuen.

Magnum Books are published
by Methuen Paperbacks Ltd
11 New Fetter Lane, London EC4P 4EE

Made and printed in Great Britain
by Richard Clay (The Chaucer Press) Ltd
Bungay, Suffolk.

Things a father should know

How to change a nappy – *and* dispose of the old one;

How to cook a meal the children will eat;

How to play, watch or at least listen to football;

How to flirt with a small daughter (very important) without making his wife feel like a discarded bedsock;

How to say "That's final" and not go back on it as soon as his wife's out of sight;

How to prize his wife's hands from the neck of their firstborn and clasp them round a glass of gin;

That Elizabethandthechildren is actually four words, not one.

Things a mother should know

How to keep the children from interfering

with Daddy's pen, electric drill or afternoon sleep;

How to yawn with her mouth shut when being told about the tailplane weakness of a Messerschmitt or what Marlene said to Lucy in the playground;

How to comfort a son without exactly saying Daddy was wrong;

How to construct a packed lunch, a shepherd's costume and a plausible Off Games note in ten minutes flat, usually while cooking breakfast;

That a man who took refuge in bear-and-squirrel talk, shared dottiness and Pooh stories, hasn't suddenly gone serious for life just because of Baby Roo;

How to know by intuition when it's the *last* button that's coming off a pyjama jacket;

How to drive a car safely with the children's hands over her eyes.

Things children should know – but don't

That grown-ups don't have *all* the fun just because they sit in the front seat and stay up after ten every night;

That re-telling a joke your elder brother told five minutes ago is no way to raise a laugh;

That Mummy does not regard "You're the oldest person in this *house!*" as a compliment;

That there's nothing in the United Nations Charter which says a child must have a Coke for every short snort consumed by a parent;

That half the world's work is done by people who "aren't feeling very well";
That Mummy and Daddy don't actually do all that *just* to make a baby.

Foulkes' Law of Random Results states that "In Parenthood (as in business, politics and war) the correlation between the efforts of the people in charge and the results — dazzling or disastrous — appears negligible."

NIGEL FOULKES

The battered parent

This is not a book about how to bring up your children properly; there are too many of them already. Childcare is a growth industry with half a million teachers, eight thousand health visitors, the National Children's Bureau and uncounted numbers of academics all toiling away on how children develop, how their teeth form, why they don't learn to read, what must be done to rid them of psychosis and nits. Scarcely a day goes by without another book on Children's Rights or Your Wonderful Baby.

It's the rights and needs of parents I'm concerned about; the battered consumers of all this expertise. For since the one thing they're all agreed about is that children are wonderful, then everything that goes wrong must be our fault. I blame Rousseau, myself: all this stuff about the nobility of the savage child, which could only be tainted by rotten old civilised us. What's surprising is not that he left his own children on the steps of an orphanage, but that he apparently did it before he saw what sort of children they would (inevitably) be. Man is born free, indeed! Man is *not* born free – he is born attached to his mother by a cord and is incable of looking after himself for at least seven years (seventy, in some cases). Before Rousseau, they believed in Original Sin, so any faint signs of redemption the child might show were deemed to be so much gain; and even in Rousseau's own time nobody took a whole lot of notice, because so many of the children died before they were grown that there wasn't much point in running a child-centred home. But his theories have now come home to roost with a vengeance.

In the thirties, mothers may have leaked their frustration down the fronts of their blouses as they waited for the clock to strike feeding time, but at least they knew they were doing the right thing. But then Spock started saying "Ease up, your child is *naturally* friendly, *wants* to behave: just enjoy yourself." This meant that every time the child was awful (just as often as before, of course) you were not only miserable because it was all going wrong, you knew you were wrong because you were miserable. There's a good deal of this Fun Morality around still, and now they've invented one that's even worse: we can do what we like – roar, scream, ignore – just so long as we love them enough. And a fat lot of good that is.

In the last fifty years we've been told to do everything with regularity (Truby King), not to bother with timetables (Ruth Millom); to put them in splints if they masturbate (Lydiard), never to check genital play (Spock); that dummies deformed the face, didn't deform the face but were dirty; that dummies satisfied the sucking instinct. We've been told to be natural *but* never to smack them, to give them a balanced Diet *but* never care if they leave it; small wonder that even when we've decided what to do, we've scarcely any confidence in doing it. I reckon the only two things I've ever got across with any certainty to my own children are the rules about road safety and chewing gum (one entirely for their benefit, one for mine); all the rest is doubt.

Maybe we're too struck with being On the Side of Youth (i.e. not as old as we feel). Maybe it's our obsession with not being

THEN THE LITTLE SPERM SWIMS WITH ALL HIS FRIENDS TIL ONE BY ONE THEY FALL EXHAUSTED AND THEN IN THE END..

authoritarian, which means you have to per-suade your child he invented 1066 for him-self. Maybe we simply focus on our children to this embarrassing extent because we've had too much time and money to do it with; but in the bad times coming who's going to be able to take an hour wheedling the creatures into the lifeboat?

We, personally, have been at it for over ten years, since the first of our two sons was born; and I'm bound to say (since you get a lull between toddlers and teenagers) that they're pretty agreeable these days. But looking back on the battlefield it seems to me that most of the innumerable things I did wrong – the arguments, the pointless ex-planations, the idiotic confrontations over things that ought to have been routine – were the result of all the good, enlightened child-centred policies I ever tried; and that things went far better when we just got on with the business of being grown-ups and let them fit in. The day on which I realised that I, too, could make a flat statement with-out giving reasons – I simply said "I don't play football" – was as good as the day I found there was protein in baked beans.

I think we're all trying much too hard, ques-tioning ourselves far too much, and taking a lot too much lying down – everything, in fact, except sleep.

There are five types, however, by whom I refuse to be pressurised any more.
The Modern Jewish Mother. A Jewish mother,

of course, doesn't have to be Jewish – she just has to be prepared to eat chicken giblets for fifteen years to send her son to college. Nowadays she lets her children desolate the house and walk all over her because it's supposed to be For Their Good. So instead of saying "I've done everything for you and yet you treat me like this!" she now says "I've done nothing for you and yet you treat me like this!"

The Professional Father – usually an education-alist. He will make you feel a moral reptile if you don't read to your child for an hour a night, but has understandably taken refuge from his eight or nine children in the arms of another. Any fool can be a good parent one day a week.

Bachelor Aunts of both sexes engaged in child-care: they will tell you, for £3.50 a copy or £5 an hour, what you should do with your children. They're quite right, of course; only they don't realise, as Ma Machiavelli used to say, that parenthood is the art of the possible.

Honest Injuns who speak with forked tongue when they say "I'm always honest with my children". They mean teenage children, with whom they are currently currying favour; nobody does it with infants. "That's lovely, darling" you say, when shown a picture of splodge. "Granny wants to see you," you say, meaning you need an evening alone. Even this hoary business about distracting – not "Don't touch the plug" but "Look at this lovely rabbit!" is dishonest – you're not pro-rabbit, you're anti-plug.

Distinguished Clubmen who can't see what all the fuss is about; they treat children "as distinguished foreign visitors whose language they don't happen to speak." They have never changed a nappy on an African ambassador.

PARENTHOOD IS NOT WHAT YOU OUGHT TO DO; IT'S WHAT YOU CAN STAND.

Nestbuilding

Plenty of people don't have a chance to tailor their homes to their children; in some ways they're the lucky ones. If the landlord won't let you throw kitchen and dining room together or knock down the partition between two tiny rooms so that you can keep an eye on a toddler while you cook, you won't in later life find there's no hiding place from *Top of The Pops*. Nothing in childhood lasts for ever, especially vases, measles, convictions about education and heights at which different appliances are safe.

To start with, the main thing you need is somewhere of a decent height to change nappies: that back-ache isn't post-natal depression, it's bending over too far. Doing it on your knee is all right only for the brief patch between the child being too small and wiggly and its being too big and wiggly. If someone wants to give you a fancy cradle, fine; but you could do better letting it start life in a carry-cot that goes on wheels to be a pram, and make up the difference in disposable cot sheets.

Most of the purpose-built nursery furniture you can buy is made on the basis that little things suit little people and big manufacturers need big profits. But solid Victorian chairs the children can climb on, cupboards too heavy to pull over, are a much better bet – and you need a decent chair in the children's room if you're going to spend any time there. Get a playpen from the start – they like them only if they're in them long before they can crawl (then they learn to walk pushing the thing across to an open fire, if you don't anchor it). For children's rooms lino's better than sisal or carpet – doesn't stain, and their brick buildings have a flat base. You don't need a children's wardrobe – pegs are fine. We've found that a piece of hardboard (about half the size of a ping-pong table) can be a raft, something to put on top of a bumpy bed to play games on, a jigsaw surface, a war-game table – *and* you can simply lift the whole thing up and carry it elsewhere if they've started making Mafeking in the wrong room.

Junk shops are now "antique" and pricey, but any big town has old office furniture; we got desks for £5 or £8, swivel chairs for £1.50; if we'd been writing it up for *Ideal Home* I dare say we would have got around to painting them up and changing the handles. The more firms go bust, the cheaper it gets

– you might even pick up an old casting couch if there's a slump in showbiz.

When you move the eldest out of his drop-sided cot, it's pointless to buy him a junior bed. When you put him in a sleeping bag on the floor to accommodate a visiting aunt the wretched woman will have to sleep with her feet half way up the wall; and your child will grow out of it at exactly the moment he grows out of all his previous clothes, ideas and hobbies and you're in no position to lash out on another. Bunk beds are fashionable, but I wouldn't buy one till you've actually tried reaching too far up to make the top one and too far down to make the bottom. You could go in for duvets, of course, but all the same there are parents within a five-mile radius of any Habitat who go round with their heads bent over like budgies from trying to read aloud sitting on the bottom bunk.

As there comes a moment when the children *don't go to bed* any more, you need an adult sanctuary – maybe your own bedroom, plus a couple of chairs and a portable TV; I know one couple that spend most of their time in their vast well-furnished bathroom; they lock the door lest the children should interrupt them in the filthy adult practice of reading in silence. You have to have one place where the ashtrays aren't smashed and the pictures used as targets; whose house is it anyway?

Insomnia's a pretty name for a girl

Political prisoners are reduced to pulp by the standard technique of keeping them awake for days; parents too, only the baby doesn't bang gongs, it just cries. And cries. And cries. I've heard it suggested that they wouldn't if they were psychologically attuned to their mothers: bosh. And a very wicked thing to suggest too, since I can't think of anything more calculated to *make* everybody un-attuned. Most babies give you a bad time for a week or two; up to three months some commonly roar non-stop at a given time in the day – often the evening – and whether you find it easier to pick them up or leave them where they are depends on things like the state of your nerves, the thickness of the wall and whether there's someone pounding on the other side of it with a golf club. Later on, you *can* run to the baby every time it cries – though if you do,

let's hope you haven't landed one of the ones
that cry from tiredness; probably you'll need
to have someone run to you every time *you*
cry if you do. When they invented on-
demand feeding, the theory was that Baby
would create his own schedule; they told the
press, the mothers, the hospitals; trouble was,
nobody told the babies and some of them
don't.

One proper night's sleep a week can make all
the difference – get father to feed it or go
home to mother. If you find you can't
get *back* to sleep after a disturbance (this
goes for older children's illnesses too) have
half a sleeping pill – it won't make you miss
the crying. If you want to haul a
wailing toddler into bed with you, go ahead
– the books are all against it, but the

Newsons' Nottingham studies showed that most people do; you won't overlay your babes unless you're both drunk and enormous. If it's an older child, you may be better off in a spirit of resignation and a warm dressing-gown playing *Snap* at five in the morning than shivering in your nightdress saying "You will be all right now, won't you?" *One* night, anyway, shouldn't knock you out.

If only one could have bedtime directly·after breakfast, it might all be less trying; the trouble is, you're whacked already. So's the child, possibly; your friends will tell you that if your brat plays up at bedtime you're trying to make him sleep too soon, but it may be the other way round: he's just too tired to get upstairs. "Bathe your child with language," says Mia Kellmer Pringle, and some of the language I've bathed mine with would make the soap blush. If they wear tights or long trousers you don't have to bath them at bedtime, and sometimes it's easier in the afternoon. Or when they're mired to the eyebrows, there's a wicked pleasure to be had from lifting the entire child, clothes and all, into the water – like stubbing out a cigarette in a fried egg.

We found it essential to start drinking *before* the toddler's bedtime, and to let them have a bit of time to play *after* we'd left the room. Before they could tell the time, we set a kitchen pinger: they could play till it went off. If your children tell the babyminder their bedtime's later than it is, think twice before you correct them. A little getting-away-with-murder may reconcile them to your going out better than anything you could actually allow. But won't they feel dreadful to-morrow? Sure – but so will you, if the party was any good.

In the long run, the amount of sleep you get will depend not on how long they sleep but how good they are at staying in their cots or beds or rooms when awake. You need teddies, rusks, books, toys – and a lock on the bedroom door. We're always being told, in this connection, that you can lead a horse to water but you cannot make him drink, and it's true. But you *can* tie the beast to the horse-trough and slope off for a quiet pint.

What size cup does he take, madam?

Once upon a time there was a Dr Offen-thrash who discovered a substance found in milk which he named Nutrient O. Babies who had it thrived and were calmer and better in later life. As it was colourless, odourless, tasteless and not detectable under a microscope, it was impossible to show which babies actually had taken any on board, but the doctor said he knew, anyway; the ones who grew up crotchety, criminal and neurotic plainly couldn't have.

There's supposed to be a magic in breast milk, too, and the stuff is doubtless good for babies. But all that the efforts of those who insist it's the only thing have done is to make anyone – any woman, I mean – who can't breast feed feel rotten about it. I bet half the people who bought Nell Dunn's *Poor Cow* thought it referred to their own inferior status as milkers.

But as with cows, some are good milkers and some aren't. In primitive life, poor milkers probably don't succeed in rearing daughters at all, so the strain dies out; here, it doesn't. What those whose cup runneth not over ought to be doing is giving thanks they live in a developed country with plenty of good substitutes where it doesn't matter one way or another. Mavis Gunther, whose *Infant Feeding** is the best book going on this, says it isn't just psychology, it's shape – and you can't buy falsies for this one.

If you do want to breast feed, that's great: it's sterile, cheap and you can't leave it behind at the last picnic place. But even if you do, it's a good idea to keep on the odd bottle – maybe with juice – once a week or so, to make weaning easier later, and to give Dad a share in the action to compensate for the fact that some of his favourite gestures now suddenly drench him with milk. If you can't stand all that squalid groats-on-the-nipple bit you can knock off when you start solid feeding with a perfectly clear conscience.

If you bottle feed, at least you know what's going in (they ought to have gauges on breasts, as on petrol pumps) and you don't have to race home from the pictures mooing painfully. For heaven's sake choose a cheap evaporated milk that you can get from a delicatessen when you run out, and don't go in for Terminal Sterilisation, which is The End. If the doctor thinks you ought to

* Methuen, 1970; Penguin, 1973.

breast feed and you don't want to, tell him you're a drug addict – you'd get the baby addicted too; and remember Dr Marvin Garshs's great dictum, that those who don't have breasts shouldn't be the ones who decide. It's the medical equivalent of the woman's remark about the Pope and birth control: "He no playa da game, he no maka da rules."

"Only those in the last stage of disease could believe that children are true judges of character."

W. H. AUDEN

Untrained melody

In the old days babies were supposed to be out of nappies by the time they were a year old. This is now regarded as impossible, so it's just as well they've invented plastic pants – two not unconnected events, in my view. If you read almost any respectable magazine or manual now, you'll be told about the children who seemed trained but later "lost the use of their habits" (as the policeman said about my mother's deranged au pair girl), though I doubt if they were ever a majority. So, we're told, leave it till the child understands what it's all about, and all will go smoothly.

Only sometimes it doesn't. The trouble is that during those first two years when the babe hasn't been using a pot, he *has* been using his nappy, possibly standing up – in other words, it's not just a question of introducing a new habit, but of breaking him of an old one. Naturally you don't talk about this, because if you're a modern parent it isn't supposed to happen – though I did hear of one father wondering if his daughter would be the only known girl to go straight from nappies to Tampax.

But I can't be the only parent to wish I'd never heard of the enlightened advice, and got going infinitely sooner. Of course a baby doesn't pee on demand at eight or nine months – but at that age he accepts a circle of cold plastic under the bottom as just one more fact about this remarkable universe; from ten months on, he's got opinions, and doesn't like anything new. Your friends, of course, will tell you that even if a child is dry by fifteen months he isn't *really* trained because he can't really control it. But what do they mean "really"? We aren't asking him to make The Decision For Christ, for Pete's sake, it's just a question of habit.

Oh but, I can hear someone saying, if I go at my little boy with a pot won't he get all uptight about his bowel movements, and holding onto things, and meanness, and grow up to be a bank manager?

To this I have two answers.

(1) Well, someone must, or the thing becomes absurd

(2) No.

Drs Azrin and Foxx have recently been going around America Toilet Training in Less Than a Day. ("What have they been doing?" my husband asked, "scaring them shitless?") The book of the same name explains the method, which is all very positive and loving – the Masters and Johnson of the W.C.

The most revealing bit, to my mind, was the number of desperate parents who had written to them with untrained children of three, four and even six (after five, of course, you stop saying you haven't managed to train her, you call it a Bedwetting Problem). If you think you can keep a straight face while you assure your tot that Granny wants you to be clean, Aunt Hilda wants you to be clean, the Wombles want you to be clean (yes, even Great Uncle Bulgarià) you might try it.

It's not 'occupation-housewife'—it's 'occupation-therapy'

No one told you, as you sank into your lover's arms that first blissful night, that the process you were starting would end with your feeling wretchedly inadequate if you couldn't stick six egg boxes together to form a cart. Keeping the children occupied is an entirely modern headache – in the good old days one used the children to mind goats or sweep floors; that long summer holiday, at the end of which, as one woman put it, "the only creative play we could think of was to send them out into the garden with spades to dig their own graves", was originally designed for harvesting – I just wish they'd revive it.

It's not that we're short of suggestions: *Where?* (the educational magazine) and *Contact* (the playgroup one) are full of the sort of suggestions that make you feel tired just to read about them: there are all these bustling, caring parents constructing dragons and rubbing brasses and classifying seaweeds – how different, how very different, from one's own listless progress round the museum dinosaurs, the token walk to the park, the final slump in front of the TV.

However, Kate Moodie, who actually edits *Contact*, is I'm delighted to say dead against the kind of play which means Daddy wrestling with the cardboard cut-out while the child, bored, wanders away; "pre-school creativity is inhibited by models and directives." She simply advocates leaving heaps of materials like feathers, gravel, boxes and old jars around and letting the kids get on with it – though she does somewhat spoil it by saying that if they have more companionship and encouragement when they're small, they're apt to be more independent later on than the ones who've been told to run away and play. Perhaps these super-parents don't do *all* of it *every* weekend – any more than there's any reality in the TV ad woman with shining hair whose children exclaim, "Oh goody, Flyspit again!"

Well, we've got to get through the weekend somehow.

1. First try the things that actually need doing – painting shelves, mending the hen-house; no need to make the unemployed dig trenches in Hyde Park if there *is* work to be done.

2. Involve them in your things – my husband war-games like a fiend with the children playing Pioneer Corps to his Montgomery;

28

IF I HEAR
ANOTHER
WORD ABOUT
MRS ROTTEN
MORRIS I
  SHALL SCREAM

maybe it's only those who are themselves musical who greet the dawn with their recorders.

3. Enlightened self-interest suggests that a little time put in at the beginning of a new amusement will give you more peace later – with a new microscope, a magic set, a new game, a weaving loom; otherwise they'll fudge around for half an hour and then give up for ever.

4. When they're really small, get into a playgroup at all costs – if there simply isn't one, round up a bunch of Mums from the clinic and start one – write to Pre-School Playgroups Association, Alford House, Aveline Street, London, SW11 5DH. Or try to get a local potter, student teacher or librarian to get something going for you, even one afternoon a week. Better than soldiering on alone.

5. When your mind's a blank there are books that help a lot.

Mother's Help, ed. Dickinson (Collins, 1972) – a bit of everything;

What to Do When "There's Nothing to Do", Grigg (Hutchinson, 1972);

Harold and the Purple Crayon, Johnson and Crockett (Longman, 1972) – to get them to draw;

Pre-School Activities, Pickering and Pickering (Batsford, 1974);

This Little Puffin: Finger Plays and Nursery Games, ed. Matterson (Puffin Books, 1969). And don't forget all those Playpads and ghastly-looking colouring books which the kids adore. As indeed, they adore so much junk: one of the funniest ten minutes I've ever spent was listening to a Hampstead father trying to say "It's *your* choice, *your* decision" in a child-oriented fashion, and at the same time make sure his child didn't spend the book token on Biggles or Enid Blyton.

6. Refuse, absolutely, to read comics aloud. They'll learn to read quicker and you'll stay sane longer if you don't.

7. In any case, don't worry; one day you'll get stuck with a French girl on an exchange scheme, and the sheer boredom of talking English to her will drive you out to every museum, exhibition, stately home, market or abattoir in the district.

Only ogres smack their lips

Should you smack? People who approve say "smack" and people who disapprove say "hit", so that shows you where I stand. *Where?* did a survey of a fortnight's punishments in a variety of families and came to the conclusion that everybody smacks; all that varies is the amount of guilt you feel about it. It's unlikely that anything so nearly universal will warp your child for ever.

On the other hand, speaking as one who has laid about her pretty freely on occasion, I can't say it's done as much good as I hoped, for the same reason it doesn't do harm: they get used to it. I knew a man who was beaten every Saturday if he couldn't do his Latin; he never did learn the Latin "but," he said with pride, "I have a wonderful resistance to pain."

What I now wish I'd done was to make smacking much more rare and awesome;

and I bet what stopped me, as it stops plenty of parents, is that idiotic remark of Shaw's about it being better to hit a child in anger, even at the risk of maiming it for life, than to strike a child in cold blood. Everyone was riveted when he said it because the current view was you should *never* strike a child in anger; but he's quite wrong. It puts the motives of the parents above the likely effects: it is *not* better to be maimed for life than have a nasty half hour with Father. And if you can only forgive yourself for smacking if you've lost control of your temper, you probably won't hand it out to best effect. It's as stupid as girls who won't use birth control because they have to pretend they're overwhelmed by passion, every time. The message that should come across is that this time he's done something really bad, like running in front of the car or making the helper cry; not just that Mummy's in a bad mood again.

And it is no good saying smugly "I never spank my children" if everyone's inwardly groaning "More's the pity."

"We all of us wanted babies – but did any of us want children?"

EDA J. LESHAN

Protein on toast and a glass of arsenic

Will those who have never had a child with a feeding problem just close the page quietly and leave us alone? Thank you.

We have no wish to be told yet again that it wouldn't have happened if we hadn't pushed food into them in the first place, or if we'd fed them better food ("'I got them into good eating habits right from the start, you see,' Liz would say; as if the rest of us had deliberately inculcated the craving for chips and ice lollies against which we feebly struggled." – Celia Fremlin). Every expert tells you just to let them leave it – except all experts who tell you they must have protein, Vitamin C, plenty of fresh vegetables. And telling us just to be casual about it is as much use as telling you not to show fear when giving sugar to a snorting and enormous horse.

We made our problem worse by having few

family meals, so I was for ever poised intensely over Baby with spoon raised; and by trying, at a later stage, to reason with them too much – which would result in remarks like "Why do I have to have an egg? We're only going to France, you don't need protein to go to France." And reading American books like Spock gave us far too fancy an idea of what children should eat.

One of my most sensible friends never gave any child meat at all till it had as many teeth as a crocodile: 'Grated cheese in his vegetables one day, an egg in it the next; a bloke with two up and two down can't make mincemeat of a chump chop as his father can."

However, telling me Not To Worry was, as I recall, the thing that made me throw the food across the room even further than my son did; so I will just suggest a few things that might help.

1. Try occasionally turning the brat's feeding over to someone who really doesn't care whether they eat or not – the mother of another feeding problem, perhaps.

2. Don't put immense amounts of loving care into stuff that will end up on the floor – open a tin and then at least it's Mr Heinz that's being rejected, not you.

3. Try setting a kitchen pinger for ten minutes for anyone under three who fools and dithers – puts a limit to the misery.

4. Swallow your pride if your child will eat anyone else's food but yours, even school

food; it may be smothered with vile gravy (main course) or the same thing only yellow (pudding) but at least it's not smothered by you. Dutifully offer to copy whatever it was he liked.

5. In a good many situations it's more important the child shut up than eat up – they can be taught that they need not swallow but must not sneer – and jolly well should, in my view. When Guinness did that ad "I don't like it because I've never tasted it" they hit a raw nerve in half the mothers in England.

'COURSE IT'S REAL TOAD. SILLY

6. Since none of us really believe our children won't grow up yellow-eyed, bandy-legged, twitching and illiterate if they miss out on the right stuffs, try swapping foods he won't eat for foods he will. As follows:

Vitamin A
Found in milk, butter, margarine, cheese, green vegetables and carrots. One good

helping of carrots a *week* is enough for requirement.

If your child won't take	try instead
milk	fruit yoghurt
	junket, blancmange
	horrible pink whips
	made up with milk,
	or milk shakes
	home-made ice
	cream
cod liver oil	green vegetables
green vegetables	cod liver oil
liver	apricots

Vitamin B

There are three important B vitamins and it's all somewhat complicated; but a few foods contain them all.

If your child won't take	try instead
liver	peanut butter
wholemeal bread	bacon
milk – as above	
pork	porridge, wheatgerm

Vitamin C

They need this fairly often, but it's very easy to come by in fresh fruit and vegetables. There is about seven times as much Vitamin C in cooked blackcurrants as in cooked cabbage, more than five times as much in guavas (a cheap tin) as in cooked Brussels sprouts.

If your child won't take	*try instead*
orange juice	Ribena or rosehip syrup

If it prefers disgusting pop, mix Ribena with soda water; or make iced lollies with the concentrated juice.

Vitamin D

Oily fish is the most obvious source of this, but there's some in eggs. You can store it, so there's no flap.

If your child won't take	*try instead*
eggs	chocolate mousse made with eggs
	custard made with eggs
	an extra egg in Yorkshire pudding or pancake
	French toast (bread dipped in beaten egg and fried) with jam on it

Most baby foods are enriched with Vitamin D and you can actually get too much of it, if that cheers you up any.

Iron

You get it in cocoa, liver, bread and wheatgerm; a pity the child would always prefer to eat carpet tacks.

Calcium

There is seven times as much calcium in river

snails as there is in buffalo milk – so there, someone's worse off than you: imagine saying "eat up your nice snail". We get ours – calcium, not snails – from milk, cheese and bread, see above for milk substitutes.

A FOOD IS NOT NECESSARILY
ESSENTIAL JUST BECAUSE YOUR
CHILD HATES IT.

IM GOING ON A MARS BAR AND COKE DIET

"Nothing is more delightful than the voices of young people when you can't hear what they say."

L. P. SMITH

If you can't behave like a lady don't behave at all

When they asked James Mason if he would bring up his second child in total, absolute, utter freedom as he had his daughter Portland he said no. "It's not that I think we were wrong," he said, "we just couldn't stand it again."

Discussions about children's behaviour tend to focus on the future: will she lose her love of flowers if you stop her pulling their heads off. If you don't now prevent him mucking up Daddy's desk, will he be writing rude words on other people's Jaguars when he's twenty (assuming he can write by then, that is)? The trouble is, it may not make any difference either way – we've all known revolting seven-year-olds grow up to be charming, thoughtful young people, and others, no less revolting, to grow up boorish and unplayable. The question should rather be: how horrible are they to be allowed to be in the meantime?

Not very, I reckon. I know most people only let their children foul up other people's things, interrupt, be rude to people in shops or eat with their mouths open from the very highest motives; they think children should not be forced into an adult and alien concept of "manners". The trouble is it's got equated with knowing about silly things like fishforks and viscounts, whereas it's much more a matter of being decent to other people.

A professor told me recently that a gathering of fifty scientists had been silenced by the blood and saddles TV of the host's son because the host (American) didn't think it was fair to make him switch it off. But it wasn't fair to the scientists not to. If your child's eating puts me off my food, it's a bit rough on me (unless I'm dieting, of course – some children are almost a diet in themselves). I'm constantly being told that I must respect a child's privacy, talk to him as a reasonable person – all right, so why shouldn't he do the same by me? I can't simply wait twenty years for the mean satisfaction of seeing him suddenly become the one who has to suffer – the parent.

Saying "Piss off" is just as much a matter of habit as saying "Thank you!" There's a world of difference between saying "Don't answer back" – which denies a child's right to reply – and saying "Don't talk to me like that" – which is a question of how he does it. One of Celia Fremlin's characters,* who had just allowed her daughter to be vilely

* In *Possession*.

rude to her, said she put up with it "because of the closer, more genuine relationships it's supposed to promote. I'm not sure if it does, really. Personally, I am much more reluctant to confide my real feelings to Janice than I would be if she were conditioned to listening politely; and less willing to sympathise with hers than I would be if she felt constrained to put them in some non-hurtful form."

Let me rub it in. I once addressed a roomful of Kenyan women and only after twenty minutes realised that each one had a toddler clamped to her leg – imagine if it had been English toddlers! But the Kenyan mother never lets her child out of her sight (or hearing) for two years, so they darned well behave themselves. Ure Bronfenbrenner has

proved that the more time children spend with their parents the better for the child – and that Russian parents, who make them behave, in fact spend much more time with them than Americans, who *think* they do – but in practice leave them in front of a TV in the rumpus room with their friends. If you want to see much of your children, they'd better be more or less fit for human company, or you won't.

I suppose you think that's entertaining

"Won't it be wonderful," my husband said as we recovered from a four-year-old's party, "when they're teenagers and it's just pot and sexual intercourse and we don't have to do *anything*?" Children's parties only work if you do everything: chaos breaks out if you leave them unorganised for a single moment. Well, it breaks out anyway, actually. "She's cheating! She TOLD her where the treasure was!" "Well, how did I know Luton was his word for wee-wee?" "I don't WANT to play ..." Thank God mine now prefer a meal and show.

If you must give a party, wear baseball padding and proceed as follows:

For birthday parties
1. Have as many grown-ups as you can co-opt to change wet pants, act as riot squad and comfort the drop-outs.

2. If it's an all-boy party, you need a hefty man to break up the fights: one little darling gave my husband a lurid bruise which took three weeks to fade.

3. A treasure hunt never fails – gold coins all over the garden, fake money round the house and they "buy" little toys from a "shop". Or simply sprinkle Smarties round the house and they fill up the tubes they came out of – one tube per child.

4. Don't try and skip going home presents, it's the only way to get them to go away.

5. Work out the music for any game before-hand – you can't do musical chairs to the Moonlight sonata.

6. Entertainers are (a) cheating (b) too expensive and (c) all booked up by the time you really get in a panic, anyway. Spend the money on gin: for you, beforehand; for you, afterwards; and for the mothers who collect so that they'll think the kids had a good party.

For other occasions

7. Give a Tramp Supper – everyone comes in rags and filthy faces and old hats, they eat baked potatoes and bits of chicken and cakes in any old order. Bliss.

8. Visiting children often gladden your heart by being as lousy eaters as your own. Save time and embarrassment by laying the table for Do-it-yourself Sandwiches – bits of tomato, ham, salad cream, egg, shrimp, cucumber, etc. and let them assemble their own.

THE MAIN PURPOSE OF CHILDREN'S PARTIES IS TO REMIND YOU THAT THERE ARE CHILDREN MORE AWFUL THAN YOUR OWN.

Presents

IT'D
BETTER
NOT BE
SENSIBLE
THAT'S
ALL

1. Small children hate parting with the present that's been bought for them to give – try and make it a duplicate of one they've got..

2. You'll save yourself misery in the long run if you don't let his idea of "my big present" build up – quite often there's no one dominant thing, and grandparents take it literally and buy an elephant.

3. Bulk buying of birthday cards, small presents for visitors or other children saves

time on the Saturday on which your child has mercifully been invited out.

4. Make sure you don't give more than one present at any one feast that involves *you* – the kind where you have to set up the weaving loom, construct the tent, persuade the cat to give a hair to be looked at under the microscope.

5. There's a lot to be said for confining presents to Christmas and birthdays, but it's a bit hard if the child's birthday is too near Christmas. Procreate only in the autumn.

6. Get them to make all their presents for grannies, aunts, etc.; shows how creative you all are; saves money.

The nineteen-inch babysitter

That white space is for all the arguments about television killing family life, reducing us to square-eyed morons, etc., etc. However, as you aren't going to get rid of the thing (are you?) you can:

1. Get two small black-and-white sets instead of one glossy one. No one expects everyone in the family to read the same book, after all, and it *is* hard to miss the last ten minutes of a thriller because of an unexpected visitor.
2. As soon as they can read, make them mark what they want to watch ahead of time. It won't *stop* them saying "But I want to watch Scooby-doo!" when it's tea-time, but it means you can get the fights over earlier in the day when you are fresher and more likely to win.
3. Stick to your guns about meals. On any

one evening, it may seem easier to lob them their beans as they sit there; but after cooking food for five years that no one has noticed or tasted you just might go out of your mind and poison them.

4. You could appoint one child as Programmer, and get *him* to sort out, on paper, who can watch what when.

5. Remember television does serve the same function as the Rum Ration used to in the Navy – something pleasant which can be withdrawn as a punishment without affecting the smooth running of the ship.

P.S. And if you do decide to End It All and get rid of the set, reflect that you'll be rid of the children too for large stretches of the day – they'll be watching on a friend's set down the road.

Taboo subject:
Sex, Money and God

American teenagers, it's said, know all about sex; they just think the money comes from God. Taboos change.

"Son, I think you're old enough now to learn a little about the grown-up side of life. Do you remember that squirrel we saw playing with the nut yesterday?"

"Yes, father."

"Well son, that nut didn't just happen to be there. It began as a tiny seed, and when it was full grown to nut size in a special place inside the squirrel's tree, it was ready to come out. Well, it's the same with people. You put a few pounds in a bank ..."

I suppose we all know what we're supposed to say about sex: it is Good, and Healthy; and given a little swift footwork with questions like "Did you and Daddy do it last night?" it's no problem provided you start early enough. After puberty it's trickier, simply because of all that mad embarrassment that is probably part of the incest taboo. Another reason for starting young is that you teach them about birth control (vital) in the context of what grown-ups do; then you don't have to decide whether telling them implies that you expect them to rush out at once and set to. The only snag about free, frank disclosure is that if you make it Just a Part of Life, they may forget it as easily as they forget everything else you tell them – and, of course, *you* may forget to tell the third or fourth child at all.

If you find it hard to keep from giggling when you explain it all, there's a splendid book called *Where did I come from?* by Peter Mayle* that is actually funny.

Money

The easiest way for your children to learn about money is for you not to have any, and then it's only too clear the jug pours out only what it contains. What's hard is to get into their mercenary little heads the idea that because Uncle James makes more than Daddy, it doesn't mean the shady old con is in any way better or cleverer. I have a speech on the Unfairness of Life's Rewards I trot out on these occasions, but as it's usually taken to refer to pocket money I can't say I get very far with it.

Perhaps our best protection, as in the old days of sexual taboos, is to insist that it's all *private*, and that Daddy does not have a

* Michael Joseph, 1974.

NO, DARLING. IT WAS DADDY NOT THE STORK

let-it-all-hang-out attitude to his overdraft. (*Overdraft*: yours; sensible response to inflationary situation. *Debt*: theirs; wicked borrowing of a whole pound till next Tuesday.) We always planned to keep the basic handout low and let them earn more cutting the grass and such; but hit the classic economic problem of the subject classes preferring leisure to money: it didn't work.

I'm inclined to agree with Shirley Conran that it's the children who only get money for sweets and treats who are the first of the big spenders, and as it will be you that has to bail them out later, there's a case for including money for socks and school dinners in the allowance as soon as possible. So what if they starve with bare feet? Think of the American who boasted his son made a dollar a week because he saved the fare and ran along behind the streetcar. "He could make ten dollars," suggested a friend, "if you gave him the taxi fare and had him run along behind that."

There is always one girl in the class who gets a fiver a week and goes to bed at midnight (she says) just as there are always mothers who swear their kids get twopence a fortnight and are in bed by six. When yours tell you other children get more (another reason for saying money's a private matter) find out what it's spent on. I know of one family that cunningly keeps up with its juniors by paying a pound a week – but 80p of it has to go in the Savings Bank. Another family has for twenty years paced inflation by basing all allowances on the current value of the Mars Bar.

Religion

Which only leaves religion as the tricky taboo. At school, we used to reckon we were in love when we substituted the name of the boy friend for Jesus in the hymns (How sweet the name of Bill sounds In a Believer's Ear); perhaps one should go through the sex books substituting the word God for sex throughout. Certainly it's no good blushing purple at questions like: Why did God make horrid things like spiders? If you mean business, you'll find yourself praying over your left shoulder as you sit stalled in a traffic jam. I'm inclined to think we complicate our lives by trying to be too truthful too soon. You can't get your own Koestlerian doubts about outer space across to a four-year-old. You say,

"Be kind to pussy" not, "You must have respect for life." You say, "You must share the chocolate with your sister" not, "We hold these truths to be self-evident, that all men were created equal ..." Very well then: this subject also needs a Beginner's Course. Because God *likes* spiders, that's why.

Skateboarding

Teachers hate skateboarding because they can't organise it, and that's something in its favour for a start. If you want your child to let off a lot of steam without hitting you or his sisters, it's a godsend. But the protective gear is important – helmet, knee and elbow pads and above all, gloves – ordinary small-size gardening gloves with leather or plastic palms are better than the fancy kind; if he wears all this the chances are he'll come home a lot less bruised than he does from football or the normal wear and tear of the school playground.

The real snag is the cost of it all – and the fact that if you let an indulgent grandparent shell out for the best there is, the chances are he'll get it taken off him by some larger lads with less wherewithal. We let our boys save up for their own skateboards, which kept the thing within bounds; but bought them the protective gear. And it's a good idea to make sure they do it in twos and threes unless you live in a wide, quiet road or have some paved area where one child can practise in peace. If you can't stop them skateboarding in the street in the gloaming, they'd better wear light-up armbands or waistcoats as well; which you can order from RoSPA; but I have to tell you they will fight like tigers not to.

A friend rang up to agree, on behalf of her son, with something I'd written singing the praises of skateboards. Splendid; could I have a word with him? No, he'd got a broken leg; yes, she sighed, skateboarding. How was *my* son? she enquired. Alas, he had a dislocated jaw. Skateboarding? No, yawning.

To travel hopefully is a feat in itself

Cars

Most people I know who drive long distances do it at night with the children doped out on the back seat. "Many's the time we've run out of petrol rather than wake the animals," one put it. By day, the great standby is food. Unless someone gets carsick (in which case Sealegs and barley sugar) I wouldn't bother with a meal beforehand – just pass out endless snacks over the back of the seat. Take something to drink as well and a wet cloth in a plastic bag; and stop at clean-looking garages to fill the tank and drain the family. Don't let them get into the car too soon when you're starting, or you'll find yourself yelling "What do you mean you don't want to go? You can always do a few drops!" across the pavement at some astounded passer-by.

Good games are: *Legs* – you score alternately

the number of legs in the inn signs: Dog and Duck is six, Grenadier is two and Shepherd and Flock is either game and set or a nasty fight. *Motorway Bingo* – make out cards with different signs, the children mark off the ones they see. *Wheels* – each person has to spot first a four-wheeled vehicle, then six, then eight and so on to twenty; fourteen's the sticky one. *Lollipop-Sucking Competition* – who can suck slowest. *Singing* – making up Limericks on town names as you pass; or a story where each person tells a chunk and leaves it cliff-hangingly difficult for the next, "And he was just falling out of the aeroplane when ..."

Let there be no nonsense about children in the front and grown-ups cowering in the back. We may not be nobler but by heaven we are *bigger*; no one can take that away from us.

Trains

Good luck if you get a seat with a table. Bring a bag of small surprises for toddlers – a little car, an old pair of earrings, a toy dog, a boiled sweet, a little pencil – not necessarily all new. For older types, bring *Travel Scrabble*, *Magnetic Chess* or *Draughts*; *Mastermind*, small packs of cards. Those big tasteless books full of dots to join, puzzles and mazes are good, and above all you need a pad and pencil for *Squiggles*, the game of games – you draw a squiggle (or a straight line, or several, or a blob) and he makes a picture out of it; then he draws a squiggle

LET'S SEE.. LUGGAGE,
FOOD..DRINK...
GAMES..FOOD..
TOYS..FOOD...
AND MORE
FOOD

and you turn it into a picture – best of all in two rather alike colours, like black and navy, so that you cán see which bit of swan or warship was the original squiggle. The *Piccolo Book of Games for Journeys** is good. If it's for a long holiday, send stuff luggage in advance, leaving both hands free for your train case, holding each child by the hand, the food bag ... as the man said, "there'll be no real equality for women till they get three hands".

Air
Air travel is fine so long as you're in no sort of a hurry; the cheaper the charter the longer the wait, usually in an over-crowded airport at a bad time of day. Reins, for toddlers, are a big help. You

* By Manley and Ree (Pan, 1972).

need everything as for trains; airports do sell things, of course – like cheap Scotch and rolled gold pen sets. Good airports have nurseries, if you're sure you're held up long enough to make it worthwhile. If a child even occasionally still sucks a bottle, bring it along; that, chewing gum and yelling its head off are the only things that relieve the popping in the ears a small child really hates.

If you have a carry cot and hand luggage, and the hostess says, "You can manage, can't you?" say simply "No." If you start struggling, she'll let you, but if you stand there immovably, she may actually have to offer the mother-and-child service as advertised.

No airline, unfortunately, has yet advertised a crated freight service for sending children.

Walking

It sounds ridiculous to mention it, but those things on the end of legs are *feet*. If you're sick of driving them everywhere, you might see if they've still got the use of them.

Two weeks of torture makes the whole world kin

First question to ask is: whose holiday is it, anyway? Does that three-year-old really need a break from the long exhausting hours at play-school? Is Father actually happier trying to swear into a high wind through the rope between his teeth than sitting in the office surrounded by fawning secretaries? (Some fathers actually are.) I don't mind doing the bracing British beach bit, anoraks and gumboots and soggy fish fingers in the Sun 'n' Sands Café, so long as no one suggests I'm supposed to enjoy it. Conversely, though I love pottering round French markets, for instance, it's no fun if I'm dragging round someone whose eyeline is at the level of the undersides of the stalls and all those straining grey French bottoms.

Oddly, I think the people who simply take the holiday *they* want, and drag the kids along, do rather well – I'm amazed how campers stuff the baby in the rucksack, how my intellectual friends march the children smartly round the art galleries; at least, I suppose, they're not feeling guilty for screaming at the children because the children aren't enjoying something that's supposed to be for their benefit.

But quite a lot of children would be far better off among their friends and gadgets and hobbies at home and perhaps a spot of extra money for outings, than plonked down in some ill-furnished chalet or being constantly shushed in hotels. If there's only one holiday going, I'd keep it for the grown-ups – they need it.

Not that family holidays can't succeed: one family descends on the local bookshops on the first day, and makes a list of all the things they'll do when it's wet, so that when it does pour with rain they don't spend half the morning arguing and then find it's too late. A seaside holiday in the sun can be relaxing with little children because there's nothing you can break on a beach – and when they're really small you can go in June, when it's cheap. The older the children are, the colder can be the holiday – things like sailing and walking and camping; which will also fit them to go off on their own at the earliest possible moment.

This usually works better if your child can go with a friend, and it's not much cop before eight to ten; but think of the joy of two weeks in your own home without the children! Make Children Happy (16–20 Strutton

Ground, London S.W.1, 01–222 0261) ought to be called Make Parents Happy. It has all the addresses of places – good and bad where children can go on their own; recommended by *Where?* are:

Colony Holidays, Linden Manor, Upper Colwall, Malvern, WR13 6PP (for older children).
Junior Holidays, 30–34 Langham Street, London W.1, 01–883 0177.
Drake's Island Adventure Centre, Plymouth (where they sleep in hammocks just like the old Navy – maybe they keel haul them as well?).
Frigate Foudroyant, c/o GPO Gosport, Hants.

I don't want to be pessimistic, but if you do go abroad take out holiday insurance, put all the children on both passports and find out

the name of an English-speaking doctor. Alida Baxter's account* of her husband trying to *mime* diarrhoea in a Spanish chemist's (and even then he only got the address of the local midwife) would not be funny if a little girl's appendix was in question.

* In *Flat on my Back*.

How much is that froggie in the window?

A pet, you think, would be educational. But don't think for a moment your children will learn the facts of life that way. Daddy Gerbils may help Mummy Gerbils through the experience of childbirth, but as they suffer vitamin deficiency if not allowed to eat their own droppings the parallels can't be pushed far; cats suckle their kittens, yes – but you'll spend a lot of time saying, "I *know* that's her father she's mating with but with cats it's different."

It's the facts of death that pets are good at: indeed you're in trouble with pets that don't die. As one mother put it, "Don't let anyone give your child a terrapin, they live too long, you may have to be getting terrapin-sitters for forty years – make them take it back and give a mouse. They smell, but live only two years." She says when they do die children may need to howl in mother's arms until they can howl no more, with no parental comment in particular. Oddly enough children, who are quite unmoved by the gory effects of bazookas on the human stomach, are very squeamish indeed about the vet's incinerator, so either give the dead friend a Christian burial or say that it is buried in the vet's garden (and remember to tell the vet to back you up).

Pets kept by people I know include: *lambs* –not recommended, they are still lying about the sofa trying to look cute when they are nearly full-grown sheep. *Big dogs* – O.K., they let little children pull themselves up by their tails and learn to walk. *Little dogs* – too much the same size; they feel threatened and get yappy and bad-tempered. Anything used as a *guard dog* is, in my view, not safe for children though, of course, as with Belloc's tiger, mothers of large families who claim to common sense may find Alsatians well repay the trouble and expense.

Hamsters aren't bad; they all loathe each other so you only need one. *Guinea-pigs* are O.K. though friends grumble loudly about the escalating cost of hay. *Rabbits* eat too much: you can have a rabbit pressed flat against the back of his hutch with green stuff and he'll still be hungry in an hour or two: only O.K. if you have a big garden or live over a greengrocer's. I have seen the *tortoise* described as a responsive pet, which reminded me of Sydney Smith seeing a small girl stroking a tortoise "to give it pleasure": "You could as well please the Dean and

Chapter of St Paul's by stroking the dome."
Also you pack them away for the autumn and
in March they may turn out to have been
dead for some time. *Budgerigars* can be
taught to speak – but only if you say it over
and over and over again every single day,
after which presumably *it* says it over and
over and over again every single day ...
Birds, anyway, die a bit quickly if you forget
to feed them and the children feel too guilty.
Goldfish get mouldy, I'm sorry to say, and
I have heard of more goldfish going down
the drain than vicars' daughters in Soho.
Cats are quite perfect.

The one thing everyone agrees on is that you
will end up feeding, walking and cleaning the
pet yourself (with the possible exception of
small girls and ponies) so don't get any pets
for the children you don't secretly want for
yourself. A surprising number of the children
who come to our house claim to be allergic
to cats. I'm not saying their mothers are liars;
just that you could try that alibi too.

Education is a drawing out, as they said to the man on the rack

There are five times to worry about school:

1. When your child hates to go to school so there must be something wrong.
2. When your child loves to go, so they can't be working him hard enough.
3. When the teachers say you ought to worry.
4. When the teachers are obviously not worrying enough.
5. When you feel like worrying about something.

In all cases, you have to tackle the teachers; whose view of us is summed up in the phrase that whoever ought to have children, it certainly shouldn't be parents. It's a jolt for a normally responsible, competent grown-up suddenly to meet people in whose eyes they are merely the cause of all that is wrong with

Smith, J. And, like the P. G. Wodehouse character forced to print his old head-master's *Some Little Known Aspects of Tacitus* in his society magazine, we all have a hangover of fear from our own school days.

I'm inclined to agree with my father (a schoolmaster) that "the main purpose of education is to keep them off the streets – the teachers, I mean" – though why, considering some of our schools, even teachers should prefer their insides to their outsides remains a mystery. But their expectations of your child are crucial.

Some researchers went into a school in California and did phoney tests, after which they told the teachers that a certain random selection of children had greater "potential" than the others. Two years later, these were indeed the children who were doing best. So if you want your child to be successful enough to keep you off the Social Security in your old age, you have somehow to sell him to his teachers now.

"Trying to make yourself interesting" in the old nanny's phrase is generally a damp squib; they only feel threatened, and if you suggest that your child is not doing as well as he should you are immediately branded as an over-ambitious parent driving your poor little numskull to the situation of B.A. (failed), when he'd be better off driving a plough. Though, as one mother tartly re-marked in *Where?* when she'd been ticked off for just that, "If ambition and achievement and academic are such dirty words one wonders how these educationalists got their jobs."

Apart from never approaching a teacher in an entirely sober condition (because of the nerves, as above) the advice I've gleaned from more practised parents is this:

1. Put everything in the form of a question – less hurtful that way. "Do you think Sarah may be getting too much needlework?" rather than "She isn't learning a thing."

2. Start off with whatever they are absolutely bound to say – this forces them to have a second think. "I know my child is bad at Maths ... writes badly ... never listens to a word you say ..."

3. If you feel the need to supplement the school with coaching or an educational assessment or a therapist (they are not all Freudulent), tell the school before you do it or never – it's as bad as telling your G.P. about this smashing faith healer you met. (Write to Mind, 22 Harley Street, London W.1 if you don't know a children's psychologist or child guidance clinic in your area.)

4. One line that never, never works is "The extraordinary thing about little X is that before she came to your school she was brilliant/advanced/miles above average, and now is strangely thick/backward/below par in practically everything. I wonder why this is?" More successful is, "It's really amazing what you've done for little X who before she came to you was thick/backward/generally hopeless and is now brilliant/balanced/generally above average; now how can we just manage to get her through her exams?" (It's a great word, that – balanced. It doesn't actually mean anything except that she is equally bad at Maths and French.)

5. If you can get to know a crucial teacher personally, you actually can pool information on your child; there's no law against asking them to a meal. But remember you *aren't* trying to do the same job. When the nursery teacher smugly pulls your screaming three-year-old away from you with the words, "He'll be quite all right as soon as you've gone" she doesn't realise

74

the screaming will stop not because she's better with children, but because one only throws rages at one's nearest and dearest.

Choosing a school

Always supposing you've got a choice, of course — too often you haven't. You ask around — but notice the source of the advice you're getting: "They were terrible to Rupert" *may* mean only that Rupert was as terrible as usual to them. Also, if all your progressive friends send their kids there it may be a darn good school but it's *those* little thugs that your children will bring home to tea. It's worth subscribing to *Where?* (write to Ace, Trumpington Street, Cambridge) and asking details of their advice service; that mag has the answers to plenty of school-choosing problems and will give all the jargon you need to talk back to teachers. Be wary of a school that's about to change its Head — though it takes about two years for any difference to show. Ask to see round — if they won't let you, that tells you a good deal to start with. Ask if there is a P.T.A. — if there isn't, you might get stuck with starting one.

Since as I've said, the teachers are the clue to the whole thing, you might as well pick a school where you can stand their style — if they are hairy types in jeans and you are blue-suited (or vice versa) you may find it hard to get on their wavelength; equally, if uniforms and school songs and keenness on the rugger pitch set your teeth on edge, it's pointless to feed your children into such a system and then waste energy hating it.

WHO ELSE WOULD TAKE YOUR CHILDREN FOR SEVEN HOURS A DAY?

Repair and maintenance

How anyone survived children before aspirins and Elastoplast I can't imagine; the one way the modern parent really scores is when it comes to what's in the medicine cupboard. My top list includes the following:

Drapolene – at first for baby's bottom, later for scratches, cuts, small burns, Daddy's bottom, a chapped mouth and any slight skin trouble you can't be bothered to take to the doctor to get a prescription for.

Betnovate – for faces but only available on prescription and it mustn't be used too continuously as it contains a cortisone.

Phenergan – baby's first booze-up. The great thing about this antihistamine, which makes them sleepy, is that you needn't be sure what's wrong before you give them some.

Actifed Co – a de-snuffler: great for colds and coughs caused by catarrh. Send a fresh helping with them to school in a tiny bottle.

Waspeze – wasps should not have been invented before this was – or any other insect either. There are other antidotes, but this works quickest and contains local anaesthetic.

Milk of Magnesia – well, you have to do something when she's feeling sick, even if it *is* only a Maths test. This can't do any harm.

Bonjela – for sore gums; stings for a minute then cuts down the ache. I wish I'd known about it when they were teething.

Antiseptic wipes – these sting like mad so clean water is better; a great help by cow-ridden streams, however.

Nail varnish remover (or acetone) – eases off Elastoplast and removes seaside tar. (Incidentally, if you rip off Elastoplast, immediately press *hard* with a finger. It's what beauticians do when they tear off the eyebrow wax.)

Question: Is it catching or is it just psychological?
Answer: Psychology is catching

The hardest thing with family illness seems to be deciding just how ill they are. Obviously we all need some sort of book (I'd choose Spock* because he gives nice short quarantine periods); and you can usually tell when a child is simply shamming; but there's a vast grey area between the shamming and the seriously sick.

* *Baby and Child Care* (Bodley Head, 1969; New English Library, 1969).

What bitches up the whole thing is that (1) what starts as jealousy, school phobia or fear of separation can go on to be a perfectly respectable physical illness – maybe Melanie did fall downstairs to get your attention off the baby, but she still needs splints for that broken leg. (2) It works both ways – a child is just as likely to be playing you up because it's tired and sickening for something, as it is to come all over peculiar because you yelled at it for standing on your handbag. (3) And – the really tricky one – even if the trouble is psychological, the best way to tackle it, psychologically, may be to behave as if it was a purely physical ailment. They say it's not the medicine, it's the spoon – but a fat lot of use that is if the spoon is empty.

A really good doctor will never just shrug anything off as a stress symptom – for one

HISTORY TESTITIS I SHOULDN'T WONDER

thing she'll make jolly sure she isn't diagnosing a grumbling appendix as school phobia. (Irving Cooper has stories of children in mental homes who were in fact suffering from a muscular disease.) And she'll realise that theories change about what *is* psychological – bedwetting was always thought to be. until so many cases got successfully treated by other means that the theory no longer (if you'll pardon the expression) held water. And she won't leave you without something to do about it – for example, she'll give a bedwetter some mild tranquilliser, which my doctor freely admits simply helps the parents and the doctor to contain themselves until the child grows out of it.

Why do I say "she"? Partly because my super G.P. is a she, so it seems only fair; but partly to emphasise that you may need a different doctor once you've got children. The witty bachelor who was such a tonic when it was just you and your hernias may not seem to know the name of the game you're playing now. If switching doctors isn't practicable, latch on to the one at the clinic. And if it's a group practice, play fair. Wait for the one who knows the continuing saga by all means if it matters, but don't insist on the busiest partner if it's just a bashed ankle or a vaccination.

Verrucas
Sooner or later your child, like Archimedes, will leap out of the school baths and rush

down the street crying "Verruca! Verruca!"
When this happens, do not muck about; go
straight to a chiropodist. Your G.P. has to
give you something mild enough for you
to apply yourself, and it may take months;
chiropodists strap on a bit of quicklime or
something (it doesn't hurt) and the whole
nonsense is over in a week or two.

Aegrotit for Aegrotat

Personally I believe that what Randel my
son in the ballad really said was, "O mother,
mother make my bed, For I must die this
morning, but I'll be better in time to go out
to tea." I never realised I had a technique
for getting only semi-sick children off to
school till I happened to use it on a grown-
up, racing round to a colleague's flat with
thermometer, sympathy, brandy and a de-
congestant and arranging for her to get to
work in a taxi.

The formula is: (1) sympathise like mad:
"Poor darling, let's see how you are after
breakfast." This gets them dressed and gives
them hope, otherwise they'd refuse to move;
(2) take temperature, to destroy moral case
for being ill at all; (3) offer strong medicines;
(4) then discuss how they're going to get to/
from school – you can offer to fetch them, as
a treat. Somehow the question of *whether*
they are going gets by-passed completely.

If they do have a temperature, of course,
you'll want to keep them home. But it's
only the child you suspect is really *not* ill who
needs to be kept in bed – to bore him

into going back tomorrow. Keep him in, certainly (however much you wrap him up, you can't pre-heat what he breathes into his lungs) but he'll be warmer dressed in a jersey in front of the T·V than hanging from the picture rail in his pyjamas.

Help!

Plenty of battered parents never think of help in the house because they assume it has to be much more expensive than it is. Of course Nannies cost a lot and make you slave round cooking for them as well; they're probably only worth it for the highly-paid working mother. Much easier are Mother's Helps who mop floors as well as tears; you can often get a motherly sixteen-year-old, though they aren't all that cheap and you do have to feed them. If you've hired them for qualitites of cow-like tranquillity you absolutely don't have yourself, it's unfair to be furious if they take an hour and a half, reflectively stirring the water with one hoof, to do the washing-up. For either of these advertise in the *Nursery World* or the *Lady*; there's also a firm called Nannies Unlimited in London, or Helping Hands (address below).

The au pair scene isn't what it was, since

the E.E.C., but there are still foreign girls; the trouble with them (as indeed with mother's-helps) is that you take on half the problems of having a teenage daughter. The children may learn pidgin English as their mother tongue if you leave them too long with the Señorita, and there *are* husbands who tiptoe to their rooms – though rather more tiptoe out to the pub from the sheer boredom of it all. The best way is to get them through other foreign girls working in the district, then they don't get so lonely. Or try putting a notice in the register of jobs at New Zealand House or Australia House. If you live anywhere near a centre of education, try students. If you just want baby-sitting, you needn't be too fussy about sex or type of study, and they may pay you a little for the room – get these through the lodgings bureau of the college concerned. If

you want, say, three afternoons a week or some help with the washing, then a male sociology student might not do; advertise for your thirty-year-old theology research student through the *Lady*, or the student magazine or union. With this, as with mother's helps, *timing is crucial*: plenty of choice in the autumn, none at all in January. If you have nerves of steel you can have a disturbed fifteen-year-old and/or unmarried mother-to-be, ask the local authority; but it's dodgy. She hates you for the comforts you've got that she hasn't – a husband, an income bracket. Might be less trouble just to look after your own – until they get to be fifteen, pregnant and disturbed, that is.

And there are plenty of people who will baby-sit or push a pram or an iron for an hour or two a day. The trick is to advertise for just what you want, no more, no less: "Woman wanted to do ironing impeded by two-year-old" or "Take my twins to the park twice a week with yours" – there's probably someone who wants just that. A great many mothers who've had a chance of both say they prefer a few hours a week of predictable freedom to the bore of having someone living in the house anyway – what they say is, "We couldn't walk around with nothing on", which I take to be a euphemism for making love on Sunday afternoons.

Final word: don't have fixed notions about age. You think of a young girl bounding to the park with a pram, but consider the ones you know. Do they bound? Anywhere? They lie on the back of their necks listening to a transistor. The spryest helper we ever had was seventy and is now an honorary grandmother – if you want a grandmother, and you can't in my view have too many, write to Adopt a Granny – Mrs Venonica Pye, c/o 54 Main Road, Tiddington, Stratford-on-Avon, Warwicks. Or ask your local paper's woman's page to do a heart-warming feature.

Consider taking a young girl on holiday (so that it actually is one, for you); getting a schoolboy to amuse sons in the hols; asking an outfit like Babyminders (if in London) for a daily nanny one day a week shared by several of you. In real emergencies, your doctor can sometimes fix up a Home Help; or you can get a helping hand from Helping Hands, 8 Strutton Ground, London S.W.1. Super emergency mothers who can cope with car, kids, cooking, the lot, come from Country Cousins, Broad-bridge Heath, Sussex (who also do holiday helps, etc.). They are good enough to be very expensive, but once in ten years they save your life.

And if you are lucky enough to get a bit of help, and some ass tries to make you feel guilty about it, remember that it's totally *un*natural for a mother to be cooped up alone with her children – never happened down on the farm. Articles in magazines saying you should be for ever with your kids were written either by a man, in which case forget it; or a woman whose children are grown, in which case she's forgotten it; or someone who has at least got her children out of the way for long enough to write that article. That may be *her* way of surviving them.

"They're just like children really." — phase used by Colonial ladies about those whom they believe to be fundamentally savage and untrustworthy.

Grown-ups of the world unite!

Collective action: Getting together with other parents to *do* something about the master who pinches their bottoms, the un-manned crossing outside the school, the hour your young consider reasonable for parties. In one town six parents of children of eleven plus rebelled against fetching them at one in the morning, so they got together and refused. Counter "But all the girls are going" with "But all the mothers are objecting."

Blackleg: Someone who plays *Monopoly* even when their child has a friend over for the afternoon.

Lock-out: What finally happens when a mother tires of her child saying "You are *fat*" in the bathroom. It's only locking them into their rooms the psychologists object to.

By now you know where I stand. Together

we must man the barricades between the nursery and the living room, between the cot and the double bed, between the sweet shop and the bar. No one person can go it alone. I reckon one must stay on the same side of the conflict as one's mate. I'm not saying there aren't occasions when a woman has to stand up for her kids against a drunken bully of a husband, moments when a man feels like protecting his daughters from the savage unreasonableness of their mother. But such tragic crises aren't the stuff of every day. Mostly, when we have to choose between what would suit us as a couple and what would be nice for the children, we're such puritans we plump for the children just because we'd rather not.

But I doubt if we should. The husband whose television is always turned to *Planet of the Apes* isn't going to enjoy home much; the woman who feels nailed to the draining board lest her children be deprived isn't going to enjoy being married and having a family. O.K., leave the kids with Gran while your mate carts you off to Spain; it won't kill them – but it might destroy you if he took someone else to Spain. All right, so your daughter isn't as fussed over as her friends, because Mum's busy at the clinic; if Mum didn't do that, she might be hating the lot of you for the trap she feels you've made for her. In the long run there are few things you can think up that will hurt your children as much as a serious rift between the two of you; don't make a human sacrifice to the great God

child, who won't be there for ever.
"One day they'll grow up and get married,"
wrote Betty Macdonald. "'Are you sure?'
said Bob hopefully."

Finally, a code for parents so that we don't
cut each other's throats by accident. We're
all on the same side, after all.

Parent-to-Parent Code

1. Never change the plan – from *Snow White*
to *Frankenstein*, say – without consulting;
it may not upset your child but it's not
fair on the father of the one who has
nightmares. Alternatively Auntie Emmie
may have been going to take him to
Frankenstein next day, and now you've spoiled
everything.

2. Forget about your old school don't-tell-tales when it comes to other people's children doing forbidden things – playing truant, walking along the railway line, playing football in the road. Tell their parents, as you hope they'd tell you.

3. Play safe in cars. Lock back doors and don't let other people's kids sit in the front until they're big enough for seat belts (which is around six stone) however anxious you may be to get rid of your own.

4. Safety again – remember that visiting kids don't know your ropes – they may *not* have been taught not to eat things in the garden, if they have blackcurrants in theirs; they may not be as nimble up the oak tree as your child. Watch it.

5. Never give a pet or a musical instrument without asking the parents first – let alone an *un*musical instrument like a drum.

6. If you've said you'll collect from school

I JUST SAID HER SAMMY COULD BE ANOTHER GEORGIE BEST AND SHE BURST INTO TEARS

or from a party, stick to it if it's humanly possible, even if your own cries off. One day it may be your turn to be told "Oh, she's going out to tea today so I won't be fetching" just as you were off to hospital or the races.

7. Don't give over-expensive presents to please your child or because you're feeling flush. Not fair on the rest of us.

8. When you tell your little boys How Babies Are Born, tell them also How Babies Are Prevented. Other people have daughters even if you haven't.

9. If your children are likely to hurl other people's clocks to the floor or heave a brick through someone else's 400-year-old conservatory, insure against the damage they may do (sometimes an optional extra on a household policy): then the sufferers will feel they can tell you just how much it did cost to repair.

10. Never leave children alone in the house unless you've checked with their parents that they don't mind; and when in doubt about this or any of the others, ask yourself sternly, "What would the coroner say?"

"The speech in praise of motherhood." P.R. jargon for meaningless non-factual first paragraph of any report.

Last thought

When you think of your children, and of
other people's, you do know which you like
best; which you'd rather have around; which
are the ones you can really stand: your own.
You must be doing *something* right.

Also available in Magnum Books

Erma Bombeck

THE GRASS IS ALWAYS GREENER OVER THE SEPTIC TANK

"Soon after the West was settled, Americans became restless and began to look for new frontiers. Bored with the conveniences of running water, electricity, central heating, rapid communication, and public transport, they turned to a new challenge ... the suburbs."

And that is exactly where Erma Bombeck's zany, poignant, perceptive and unique book takes us: into the new heartland where a man's lawn is prized like his life, television disease has attained epidemic proportions, bare navels are out in school, the washer repairman never comes but the insurance salesman is never far away, and the grass is always greener over the septic tank.

Jilly Cooper

SUPER MEN AND SUPER WOMEN
Her brilliantly funny guide to the sexes

Whatever their grading, Super Man or Slob, Super Woman or Slut, Jilly submits them all to remorseless scrutiny. In public and private, home, office or bed, none escapes her beady eye – from guardsmen to gigolos, debs to divorcees, stock-brokers to sex fiends, tarts to Tory ladies.

WORK AND WEDLOCK
Jilly Cooper's shrewd and hilarious guide to survival at the office and in marriage

Whether your particular enemy is the Office Boss or the Office Bully, the Little Home-Breaker or the Office Crone, Jilly's outrageously funny guide to the hazards of working life is a must for you. And when she turns to the Home Front, spouses and prospective spouses would be unwise to neglect her tactical briefings. Bed, Money, In-Laws, Affaires – you name it, Jilly puts her finger on it.

More top humour available in Magnum Books